Family Fun and Games

Family Home Evening Games Based on

THE PLAN OF SALVATION

ISBN: 1-55517-840-5
e.1

Published by Cedar Fort Inc.
www.cedarfort.com

Distributed by:

Cover design by Nicole Williams

Printed in the United States of America
10 9 8 7 6 5 4 3 2 1

Printed on acid-free paper

Family Fun and Games

Family Home Evening Games Based on

THE PLAN OF SALVATION

Written and Illustrated by Melanie Millett

CFI
BOOKS
Springville, Utah

Table of Contents

Family Fun and Games

Family Home Evening Games Based on
THE PLAN OF SALVATION

Each game in this book is designed for use during your Family Home Evenings. All instructions to make and play each game are included. Each picture is full size and ready to copy. Each game features a different gospel principle included in our Heavenly Father's plan of salvation. As you include these games in your Family Home Evening, teach each gospel principle so each member of your family understands that principle. Enjoy and have fun playing each game!

Written and Illustrated by Melanie Millett

PLAN OF SALVATION CHINESE CHECKERS

LESSON: A lesson for your Family Home Evening to go with this game should be based on the plan of salvation. Discuss each aspect of Heavenly Father's plan for His children. This game represents the things that we need to do here on earth to be able to return to our Heavenly Father. Discuss with your family each of the topics on the playing pieces and how each one relates to the plan of salvation.

TO MAKE: Make 2 copies of each of the game board pages on white or colored card stock. Cut out the 4 pieces of the board and tape together to form the board as shown below. Copy the cloud onto 6 different colors of card stock and cut out. Copy the sheet of playing pieces on the same 6 colors of card stock you used for the clouds and cut out each circle. Or copy the playing pieces onto white card stock and then color each of the 6 sets with different colored backgrounds to match the cloud colors. Laminate all parts of the game for longer use.

TO PLAY: This game is played like Chinese checkers. Use a different colored cloud for each person playing. There are enough playing pieces to allow for up to 6 players. Place a different colored cloud on each side of the game board. Place all of the matching colored playing pieces on each corresponding cloud. If you are not playing with 6 players, still it is helpful to put all the clouds in place. Doing so gives the players a place to put all of their playing pieces when they get across the board. Start with the youngest member of your family. Take turns moving your playing pieces across the board. A player can move one space at a time or jump a piece in front of it, as long as the piece follows the direction of the spaces. A succession of jumps can be made if there is a path to follow. Once a playing piece reaches the opposite edge of the board, a jump can be made on the following turn to place it onto the cloud. The first player to move all playing pieces to the cloud on the opposite side of the board wins.

Sample of finished game board

GAME BOARD

Copy this and the following page twice onto either white or colored card stock. Cut out each part of the board, place the dotted lines together, and tape in place to form the compete game board as shown on the direction page. Laminate for longer use.

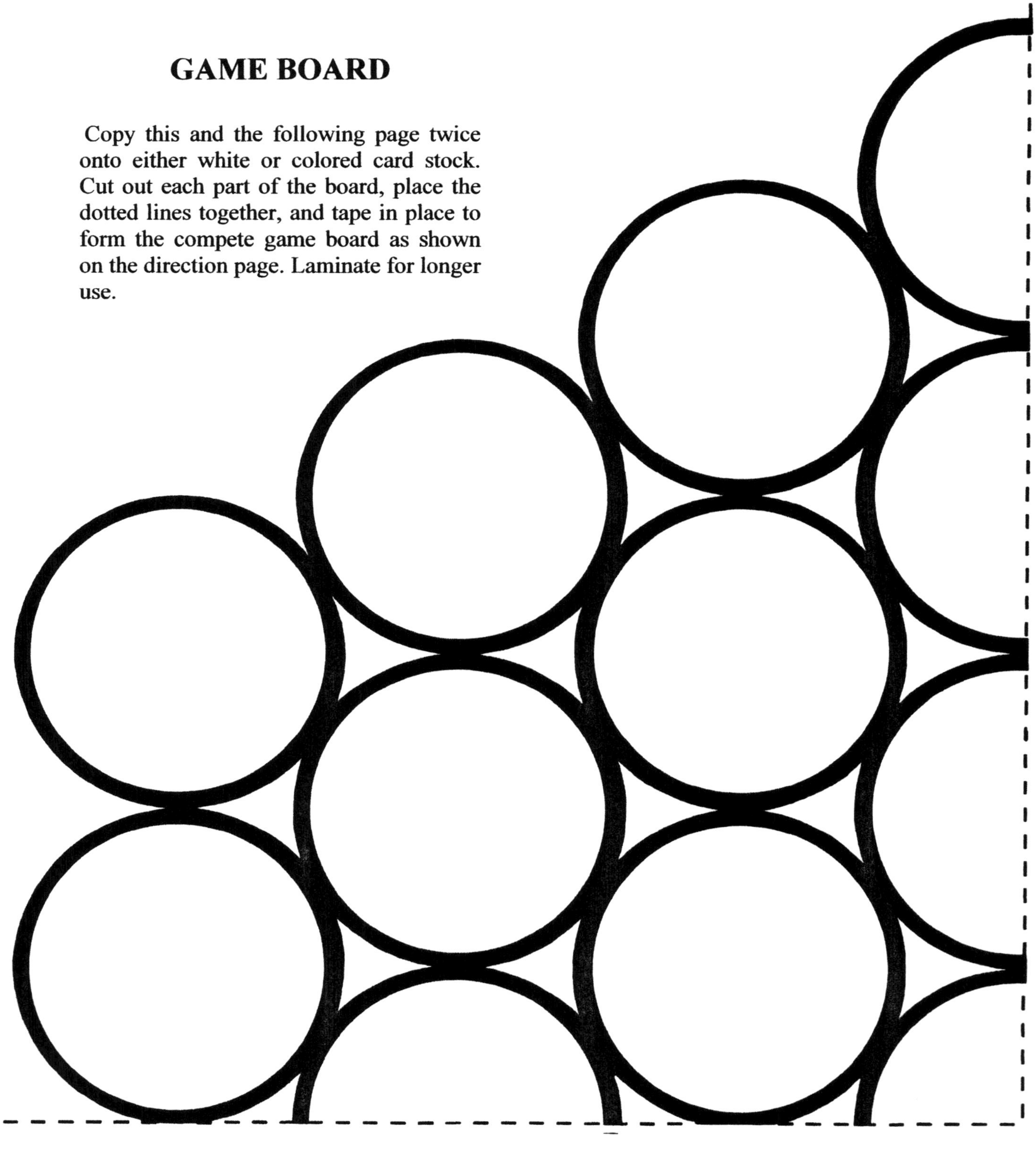

GAME BOARD

Copy this and the previous page twice onto either white or colored card stock. Cut out each part of the board, place the dotted lines together, and tape in place to form the compete game board as shown on the direction page. Laminate for longer use.

CLOUDS

The clouds are used to represent the pre-earth life, and returning to live with Heavenly Father. Copy this page onto 6 different colors of card stock. Cut out and laminate for longer use.

PLAYING PIECES

Copy this page onto 6 different colored pieces of card stock, or copy 6 times on white card stock. If using white card stock, color each picture. So each person's set of playing pieces will be different, color a different colored background for each set to match the color of clouds you have. Cut out each playing piece and laminate for longer use.

BODY BUILDING GRAB BAG

LESSON: The lesson for your Family Home Evening to go with this game should be about receiving a body and being tested. Compare the differences between what a new born baby can do with its body and a Primary age child can do with theirs. Let the children name all of the things they have to learn as a baby. Explain to your children that as we grow we have to learn to control our bodies. Then compare how following gospel principles helps our spirit learn to control our bodies to choose the right. Compare the training that a body builder goes through as they build a strong muscular body, and how it is similar to training your body to choose the right. It takes just as much hard work to learn to make the correct choices, to develop strong character and spirit, asit does to develop strong physical muscles. Discuss with your family each card while playing the game and how it will either help or hurt your ability to develop a strong spiritual body.

TO MAKE: Copy the following page on white card stock, color, and cut out. Mount the picture onto the front of a paper bag. Copy the page of Body-Building cards onto card stock. Colored paper can be used for a brighter game. You can copy this page more than once; it all depends on how many bonus cards you want to have in your game. Cut out each card. Copy the following pages of cards onto card stock. You might want to copy the good choices on one color and the bad choices on another. Cut out each card. Laminate all the cards for longer use. Place all the cards in the paper bag.

TO PLAY: Either divide into 2 teams, or play as individuals. Take turns reaching into the paper bag drawing out a card. The player gets 1 point if it is a good-choice card. The player gets no points if it is a bad choice card. If a Body-Builder card is drawn, the player gets 2 bonus points. As you pull out each card, discuss the effect the choice will have on your spiritual development. Continue playing until all of the cards have been drawn out of the paper bag. The player or team with the most points at the end of the game wins.

I gossiped about someone else

My feet walk quietly in the church

I lied to my mother

I obey the Word of Wisdom

PICTURE FOR THE PAPER BAG

Copy this page on white card stock, color, and cut out.
Glue or tape this picture onto the front of a paper bag.

BODY-BUILDING BONUS CARDS

Copy this page onto card stock. Colored paper can be used for a brighter game. You can copy this page more than once; it all depends on how many bonus cards you want to have in your game. Cut out each card. Laminate for longer use. Place all the cards in the paper bag.

GOOD-CHOICE CARDS

Copy this page of cards onto card stock. You might want to copy the good choices on one color and the bad choices on another. Cut out each card. Laminate all the cards for longer use. Place all the cards in the paper bag.

I say my prayers each morning and each night	**I sit reverently in church**	**I am polite and kind to others**
I only watch good TV shows and movies	**I have clean thoughts**	**I read my scriptures**
My feet walk quietly in the church	**I never take the Lord's name in vain**	**I fold my arms and bow my head during prayer**

GOOD-CHOICE CARDS

Copy this page of cards onto card stock. You might want to copy the good choices on one color and the bad choices on another. Cut out each card. Laminate all the cards for longer use. Place all the cards in the paper bag.

I listen and obey my parents	**I listen to my teachers at church**	**I pay my tithing**
I go to church each Sunday	**I am helpful to others**	**I obey the Word of Wisdom**
I share with others	**I am a good example to others**	**I am always honest**

GOOD-CHOICE CARDS

Copy this page of cards onto card stock. You might want to copy the good choices on one color and the bad choices on another. Cut out each card. Laminate all the cards for longer use. Place all the cards in the paper bag.

I get plenty of rest at night	I forgive others	I helped without being asked
I keep a journal	I do my best in school	I always try to choose the right
I listen to good music	I keep a positive attitude	I follow the prophet's teachings

BAD-CHOICE CARDS

Copy this page of cards onto card stock. You might want to copy the good choices on one color and the bad choices on another. Cut out each card. Laminate all the cards for longer use. Place all the cards in the paper bag.

I told a dirty joke	**I didn't say my prayers**	**I spent my tithing money on a candy bar**
I didn't go to church	**I was noisy during the sacrament**	**I am unkind to my brother**
I lied to my mother	**I didn't come home when my Mom told me to**	**I complained about having to help**

BAD-CHOICE CARDS

Copy this page of cards onto card stock. You might want to copy the good choices on one color and the bad choices on another. Cut out each card. Laminate all the cards for longer use. Place all the cards in the paper bag.

I didn't share with my friends	I talked back to my Mom	I took a candy bar without paying for it
I didn't forgive my sister when she said she was sorry	I stayed up too late and was ornery and tired the next day	I was rude to my friend
I gossiped about someone else	I didn't keep my promises	I listened to music with bad language in it

BAD-CHOICE CARDS

Copy this page of cards onto card stock. You might want to copy the good choices on one color and the bad choices on another. Cut out each card. Laminate all the cards for longer use. Place all the cards in the paper bag.

I didn't help my dad with the yard work	I didn't participate in family home evening	I smoked a cigarette
I wasn't reverent during church	I took the Lord's name in vain	I hit my sister
I didn't listen and participate in primary	I was a bad example to my younger brother	I don't study the scriptures

JESUS' EXAMPLE LADDER TO SUCCESS

LESSON: A lesson for your Family Home Evening to go with this game should be based on the example that Jesus set for each of us. Discuss stories about Jesus and how he set an example for each of us to follow. Some examples can be Jesus working as a child with Joseph, his baptism, his teaching the gospel, and so forth. Discuss how the example we set will affect other people's lives. During the game discuss each choice that is drawn to determine whether you would be setting a good or bad example.

TO MAKE: Copy the following page onto card stock for as many players as you will have playing the game. You can either copy it onto white or colored card stock. If you copy it onto white, color each ladder and Jesus. If you choose to copy it onto colored card stock, you can have a different colored ladder for each member of the family. Cut out each ladder, making sure you cut around Jesus. Cut out each window of the ladder. Fold the ladder so the side flaps go around to the back. Tape the 2 side flaps in the back, leaving the top and bottom open. Next, go to page 17 and make 1 white strip and 1 colored strip for each ladder. Copy this page of strips onto both white and colored card stock. You can choose to have a different colored strip of paper for each game piece, or use the same color for each family member. Copy the page of word strips onto white or colored card stock and cut apart. Lamination of all game pieces will help the game last longer. Thread a white and a colored strip of paper through each ladder. Make sure the white strip is on top so it shows through the windows in the ladder. Pull the strips up so there is nothing hanging out of the bottom. The white strip of paper will be pulled up as you play the game so that more and more of the colored strip will show through the windows of the ladder.

TO PLAY: Give each family member a ladder with the paper strips threaded through. Put all of the word strips into a bowl to be drawn from. Starting with the youngest member of the family, take turns drawing a word strip from the bowl. Discuss each word strip as it is drawn. If the word strip is setting a good example the family member who drew it gets to pull their white strip of paper up so that one window in the ladder shows color. If it is a bad example they don't get to do anything. Take turns with each family member. The first person who fills a ladder with color up to Jesus wins the game.

LADDER TO CHRIST

Copy this page on either white or colored card stock as many times as needed. Color and cut out. Cut out each window section. Laminate at this point so each window will have lamination covering it. Fold the flaps to the back as shown. Thread both a white and colored strip of paper through each ladder with the white one showing through the windows.

Fold this flap to the back

Cut out this area

Cut out this area

Cut out this area

Cut out this area

Cut out this area

Cut out this area

Cut out this area

Fold this flap to the back

Fold this flap to the back

Cut out this area

Cut out this area

Cut out this area

Cut out this area

Cut out this area

Cut out this area

Cut out this area

Fold this flap to the back

WHITE AND COLORED STRIPS OF PAPER

Copy this page on both white and colored card stock. You will need 1 white and 1 colored strip of paper for each ladder. Cut out and laminate. Thread both a colored and a white strip through each ladder with the white one on top showing through the windows in the ladder.

EXAMPLE WORD STRIPS

Copy this page on either white or colored card stock. Cut apart. Laminate for longer use. Place in a bowl for drawing.

I help my mom set the table at dinner time	Write a letter to a missionary in our ward	I spent my tithing money on candy	I cheated on a test at school
I read a book to my younger brother	I hold the door for those behind me	I talk rude to others	I smoked a cigarette
I listened and answered questions in Primary	I only watch TV shows that are appropriate	I made fun of someone else	I teased my little brother
I told my older sister that I loved her	I go to church each Sunday	I don't do my homework	I crowded ahead in line
I shared my toy with a friend	I fast and pray on Fast Sunday each month	I told a dirty joke to my friend	I wore my sister's blouse without asking
I paid tithing on the money I earned	I save money for my missionary fund	I was mad and frowned the whole day	I yelled at my mother
I came the first time my mother called me	I weed the garden without being asked	I pulled my sister's hair	I didn't help my dad shovel the walks
I made my bed when I got up in the morning	I go to bed on time each night	I didn't share my toys with my friends	I ignored my mom when she called me
I helped my friend study for a test at school	I write in my personal journal	I laughed out loud during the sacrament	I look at websites I shouldn't
I helped an older lady with her groceries	I say the family prayer	I didn't go on a mission	I don't go to church on Sunday
I read my scriptures every day	I baby-sit for the neighbor for free	I took a toy away from my brother	I came home over an hour late
I do my homework without being told	I only listen to good music	I took the Lord's name in vain	I didn't help my sister do the dishes
I gave the lesson in Family Home Evening	I am reverent during Primary	I dress immodestly	I hogged the ball when playing with my friends
I think of Christ during the sacrament	I made some cookies for an elderly neighbor	I didn't study for a test at school	I skipped school
I include a lonely girl during recess	I say I am sorry if I do something wrong	I disobeyed my parents	I took something that didn't belong to me
I share my candy bar with my little brother	I forgive others	I listen to inappropriate music	I didn't pay attention in Primary
I bear my testimony on Fast Sunday	I keep my room clean	I made a promise and didn't keep it	I don't care about others feelings
I visit a sick friend	I keep the word of wisdom	I gossip about others	I shoplifted

FAMILY MEMBERS CARD GAME

LESSON: A lesson for your Family Home Evening to go with this game should be based on the family. Discuss how each member of the family is important. Teach why showing love at home is important. Include teaching about being sealed together as a forever family.

TO MAKE: Copy each page of this game 4 times onto either white or colored card stock. If using white card stock, color each card. Cut out each card and laminate for longer use.

TO PLAY: As you get ready to play this game, show each of the cards and discuss with your family the importance of each family member shown. Talk about your family's different grandparents, aunts, uncles, and so forth, and how special each one is. Teach the importance of the temple card and how the temple can seal your family together forever. Also talk about the importance of always showing love to each family member whether they live in the same house or not. This game can be played as Go Fish, Rummy, Old Maid, and Concentration. Follow the rules as you would for each of the games. For the Old Maid game, take out all but one of the temple cards to use as your Old Maid card. The only difference to this game is the player ending up with the temple card at the end of the game is the winner, not the loser! This is a fun, easy game even for the youngest family members. Little children love to make matches as they play games such as Concentration or Go Fish.

FAMILY MEMBER CARDS

Copy this page of cards 4 times onto colored or white card stock. Color, cut out and laminate.

Dad

Mom

Big Brother Brent

Big Sister Sue

Little Brother Bobby

Little Sister Sally

Baby Bonnie

Cousin Crissy

Cousin Curt

.FAMILY MEMBER CARDS

Copy this page of cards 4 times onto colored or white card stock. Color, cut out, and laminate.

LATTER-DAY PROPHET BINGO

LESSON: A lesson for your Family Home Evening to go with this game should be based on how we are blessed today with living prophets. Teach how Jesus Christ restored the gospel to the earth through Joseph Smith. Talk about the importance of having living prophets and how we should always listen and obey their teachings. As you play this game, try to learn the name of each prophet.

TO MAKE: Copy each page of this game on a different colored piece of card stock. Copy the first sheet 2 times. On the second copy of the first sheet, cut out the square for each prophet. Use these to draw out a different prophet for each play of the game. This game can be played with up to 10 players. Laminate each sheet for longer use. Each playing card is different so that no one will not get a bingo at the same time.

TO PLAY: Give each family member a bingo card. Place the squares that have been cut out with each of the prophet's pictures on them into a bowl. Draw out one prophet for each turn. Smaller children might need help to find each prophet. The square with the words can either be used as a free space or drawn as all the other pictures. The person with the first bingo is the winner. You can use different things such as buttons or small pieces of paper as markers on the cards, marking each prophet picture as it is drawn. For extra fun use something like M&M's, cold cereal, or marshmallows so they can be eaten after the game is over.

Latter-Day Prophet Bingo

Latter-Day Prophet Bingo	 Joseph Smith	 Brigham Young	 John Taylor
 Wilford Woodruff	 Lorenzo Snow	 Joseph F. Smith	 Heber J. Grant
 George Albert Smith	 David O. McKay	 Joseph Fielding Smith	 Harold B. Lee
 Spencer W. Kimball	 Ezra Taft Benson	 Howard W. Hunter	 Gordon B. Hinckley

Latter-Day Prophet Bingo

Latter-Day Prophet Bingo

Latter-Day Prophet Bingo

Latter-Day Prophet Bingo

George Albert Smith

Lorenzo Snow

Brigham Young

Joseph F. Smith

David O. McKay

Wilford Woodruff

John Taylor

Joseph Smith

Heber J. Grant

Howard W. Hunter

Ezra Taft Benson

Harold B. Lee

Gordon B. Hinckley

Spencer W. Kimball

Latter-Day Prophet Bingo

Joseph Fielding Smith

Latter-Day Prophet Bingo

 Ezra Taft Benson	 Joseph F. Smith	 David O. McKay	 Lorenzo Snow
 Joseph Smith	 Harold B. Lee	 Heber J. Grant	 Joseph Fielding Smith
 Brigham Young	 Gordon B. Hinckley	 John Taylor	 Wilford Woodruff
Latter-Day Prophet Bingo	 Howard W. Hunter	 Spencer W. Kimball	 George Albert Smith

Latter-Day Prophet Bingo

 Joseph F. Smith	 Joseph Smith	 Heber J. Grant	 Wilford Woodruff
 Harold B. Lee	 Ezra Taft Benson	 Brigham Young	 Joseph Fielding Smith
 Spencer W. Kimball	Latter-Day Prophet Bingo	 David O. McKay	 Lorenzo Snow
 George Albert Smith	 John Taylor	 Howard W. Hunter	 Gordon B. Hinckley

Latter-Day Prophet Bingo

Latter-Day Prophet Bingo

 David O. McKay	 Lorenzo Snow	 Joseph Fielding Smith	 Joseph Smith
 Howard W. Hunter	 Wilford Woodruff	 Spencer W. Kimball	 Joseph F. Smith
 John Taylor	 Ezra Taft Benson	 Brigham Young	 Gordon B. Hinckley
Latter-Day Prophet Bingo	 George Albert Smith	 Heber J. Grant	 Harold B. Lee

Latter-Day Prophet Bingo

 Joseph F. Smith	 Joseph Fielding Smith	 Ezra Taft Benson	 Spencer W. Kimball
 Harold B. Lee	 David O. McKay	 Howard W. Hunter	 Gordon B. Hinckley
 Joseph Smith	 John Taylor	Latter-Day Prophet Bingo	 George Albert Smith
 Wilford Woodruff	 Brigham Young	 Lorenzo Snow	 Heber J. Grant

PUT ON THE ARMOR OF GOD

LESSON: The lesson for your Family Home Evening to go with this game should be based on Ephesians 6:10-18. These verses talk about putting on the "Armor of God" to stand firm and protect yourself in the spiritual battle against Satan. As the Apostle Paul looked at a Roman soldier who was assigned to guard him, he reminded us that our battles in this life were not physical, but spiritual. He then used the Roman soldier to illustrate the spiritual truth that God has given us spiritual armor to protect ourselves. Discuss the importance of protecting yourself from the evils of the world. Describe each piece of armor and what it represents. Help your children understand that if they put on the "Armor of God" it will help them to choose the right and obey the commandments.

TO MAKE: Copy the children on the following pages onto white card stock. Copy 1 of the appropriate gender for each member of the family. Color each picture and laminate for longer use. Copy enough of the following pages of armor so that each player will have a full set of armor. Copy them on white card stock, color, cut out, and laminate. Copy the die onto white card stock. Color each picture and cut out. Fold the die in the appropriate places and tape or glue into place.

TO PLAY: Give each family member either a boy or girl, depending on their gender. Start with the youngest member of your family. Take turns rolling the die to acquire the armor pieces. To get both of the sandals, it will need to be rolled twice. If you roll other pieces of armor more than once, skip your turn and go to the next player. The first person in the family to complete a full set of armor is the winner.

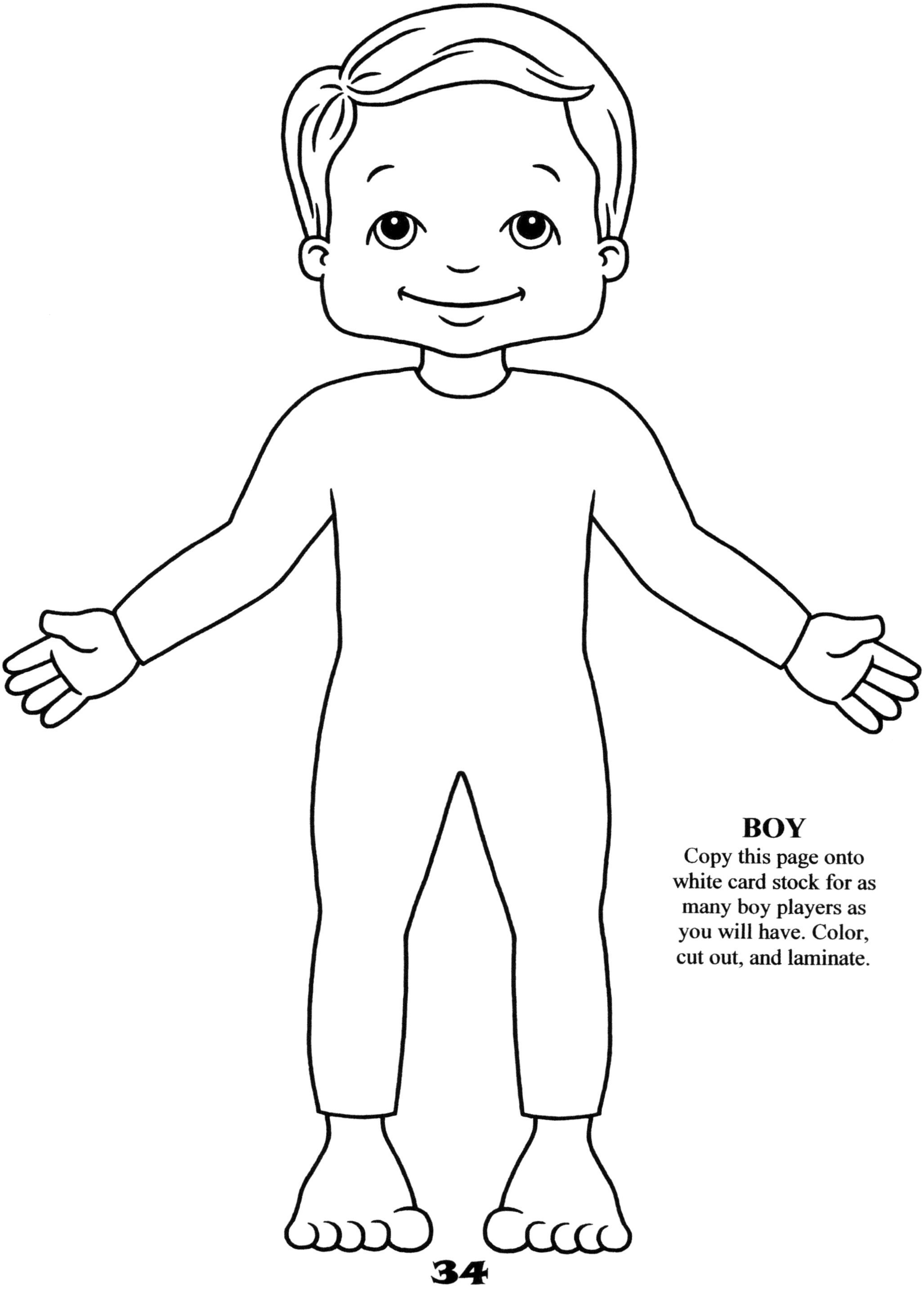

BOY

Copy this page onto white card stock for as many boy players as you will have. Color, cut out, and laminate.

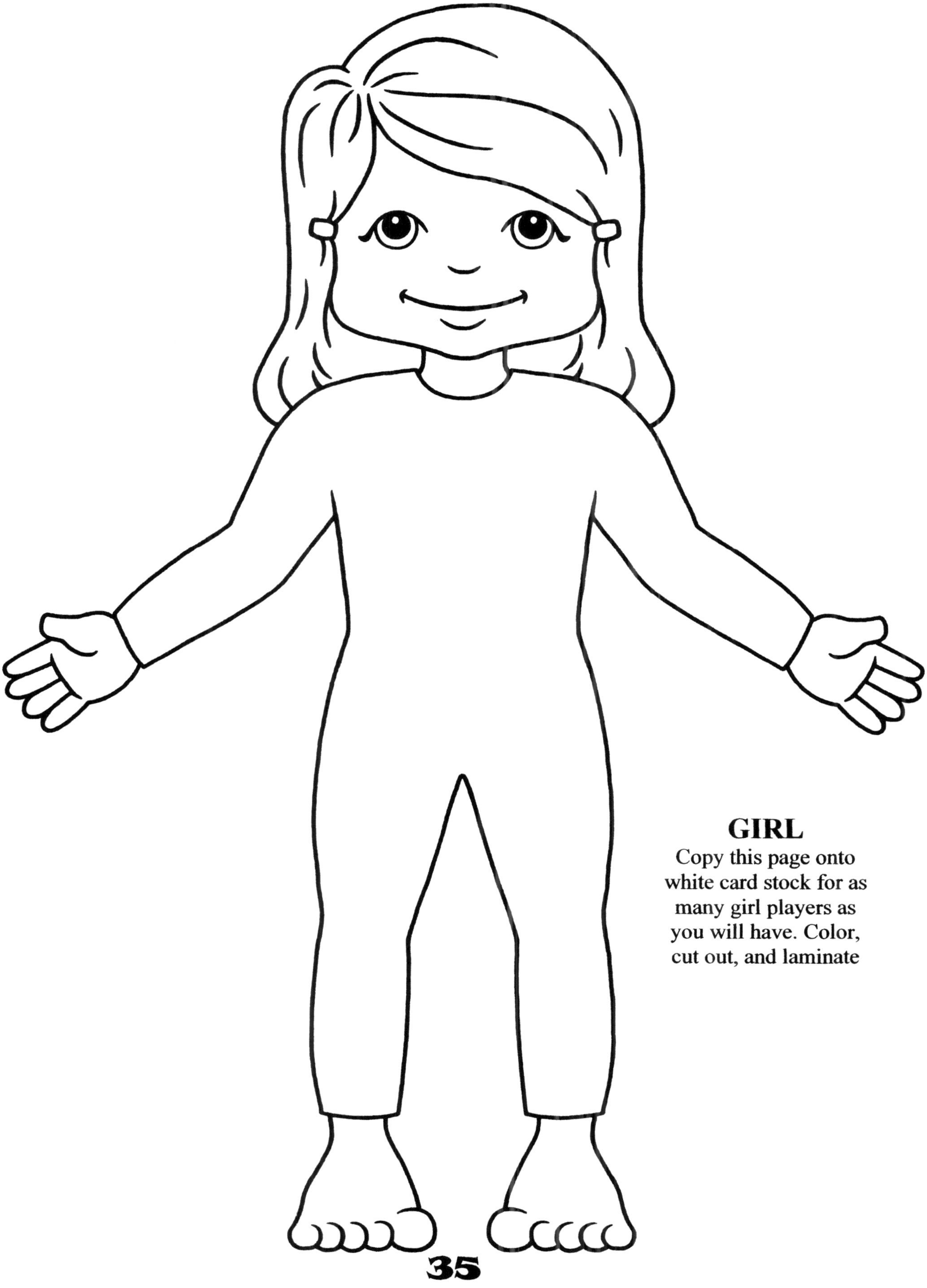

GIRL

Copy this page onto white card stock for as many girl players as you will have. Color, cut out, and laminate

ARMOR

Copy this page onto white card stock for as many players as you will have. Color, cut out, and laminate each piece of armor.

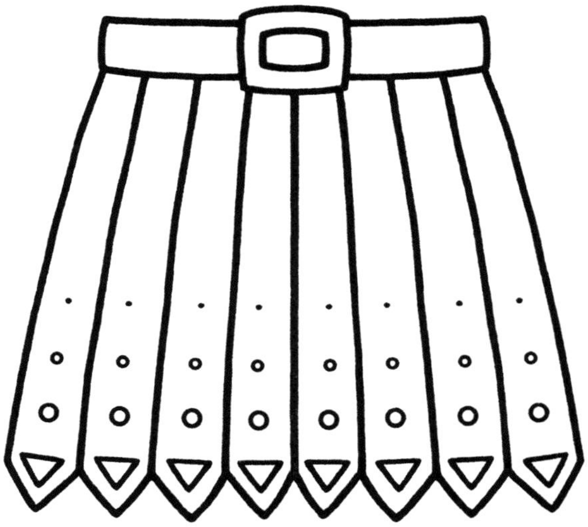

GIRD YOUR LOINS WITH TRUTH

This is a belt that holds the sword's sheath. It has an apron made of leather straps that are weighted with metal so that it will protect your thighs, hips, and lower abdomen.

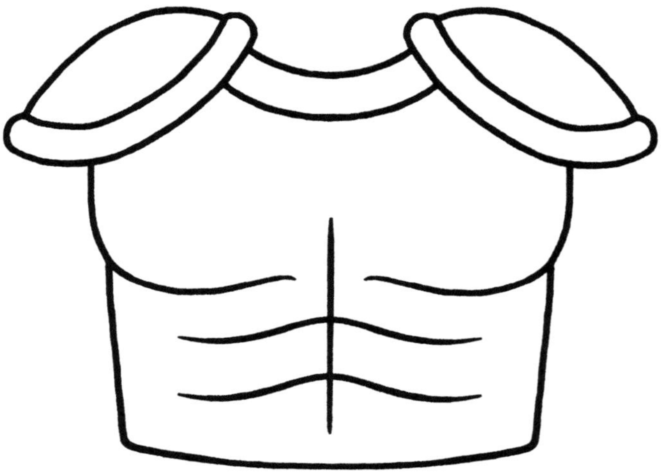

BREASTPLATE OF RIGHTEOUSNESS

This is a metal covering that will cover your chest to protect your vital organs such as your heart and lungs. This piece of armor covered and protected both the front and the back.

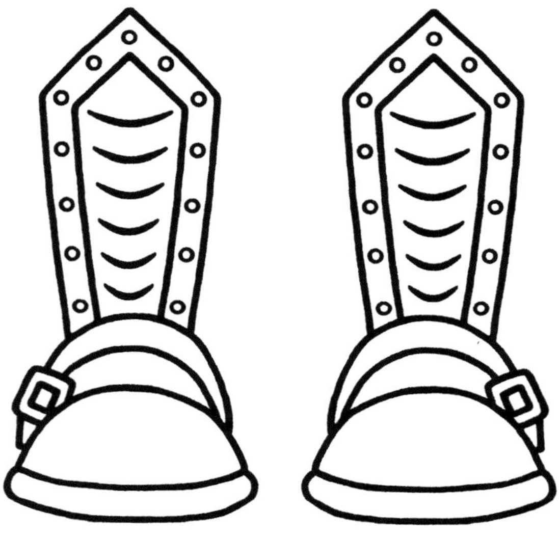

SHOD YOUR FEET WITH THE GOSPEL OF PEACE

These sandals were made to protect your shins as well as cover your feet. Hobnails on the soles of the sandal helped to keep a firm footing on slippery ground.

ARMOR

Copy this page onto white card stock for as many players as you will have. Color, cut out, and laminate each piece of armor.

TAKE UP THE SHIELD OF FAITH

This shield was made by stretching well-oiled leather over a wood frame. The oil was used to keep it soft so it could be formed to the frame. Before battle it was watered down so that as flaming arrows hit it, they would not ignite.

ARMOR

Copy this page onto white card stock for as many players as you will have. Color, cut out, and laminate each piece of armor.

HELMET OF SALVATION

The helmet was made of metal. Cheek plates and a visor were attached to the helmet to protect the face during battle.

SWORD OF THE SPIRIT

The double-edged sword was made out of strong metal. It was used for Hand-to-hand combat.

DIE

Copy this page onto white card stock. Color, cut out, and laminate. Fold on the lines and tape together to form the die.

BAPTISM CARD GAME

LESSON: The lesson for your Family Home Evening to go with this game should be based on the principles of repentance, baptism, and the sacrament. Discuss each topic and the importance of each. Look at all the pictures on the cards and talk about each one.

TO MAKE: Copy each page of this game 4 times onto either white or colored card stock. If using white card stock, color each card. Cut out each card and laminate for longer use.

TO PLAY: As you get ready to play this game, show each of the cards and discuss with your family the importance of each picture shown. Discuss how all of the pictures relate to each other and to the theme of baptism, repentance, and the sacrament. This game can be played as Go Fish, Rummy, and Concentration.

BAPTISM CARDS

Copy this page of cards 4 times onto colored or white card stock. Color, cut out, and laminate.

BAPTISM CARDS

Copy this page of cards 4 times onto colored or white card stock. Color, cut out, and laminate.

BAPTISM CARDS

Copy this page of cards 4 times onto colored or white card stock. Color, cut out, and laminate.

HOLY GHOST HIDE AND SEEK

LESSON: The lesson for your Family Home Evening to go with this game should be based on the Holy Ghost. Teach that the Holy Ghost is the third member of the Godhead. Teach your children that at the age of 8 they can be confirmed and receive the gift of the Holy Ghost. Discuss the importance of obeying the commandments so that the Holy Ghost will be your constant companion. Tell your family that the Holy Ghost can guide, warn, protect, and comfort you in times of need.

TO MAKE: Copy the picture for this game. Color, cut out, and laminate for longer use.

TO PLAY:

Part 1: Choose one person to leave the room. Hide the picture somewhere in the room. Tell everyone in the room to whisper incorrect hints. Before letting the person back into the room, blindfold them. Tell him/her that they will be hearing many voices giving hints on how to find the picture, but they may not be correct hints. As a result, the picture will be hard to find. Talk to your family about how, if we are not living correctly and have other things tempting us, we will not have the Holy Ghost with us. Being without the Holy Ghost is like being blind without any help.

Part 2: Have one person leave the room. Hide the picture somewhere in the room. Turn on your television loudly. Also turn on other noisy appliances, so it is hard to hear. Choose a second person to whisper correct hints while staying seated as the first person comes back into the room and looks for the picture. No blind fold is needed this time. Have the person look for the picture by listening to hints being whispered by the second person. After the picture is found, discuss how hard it was for the first person to hear whispered hints. Compare this to how we can become distracted with worldly things and unable to hear what the Holy Ghost is telling us.

Part 3: Now choose another person to leave the room. Hide the picture again. Choose another person to whisper correct hints. Before letting the first person back into the room, blindfold them. This time, as you let the person back into the room, have the person whispering the hints right by their side, lightly guiding them, by holding on to them and whisper which direction to go. Once the picture is found, discuss with your family that if they are living correctly this is exactly how the Holy Ghost will help them. He will be right there at our side guiding and directing us throughout our life. We won't be able to see him, but we can feel his presence and influence to choose the right.

Part 4: To include music in your lesson, choose another person to leave the room. Hide the picture again. This time, as the person is let back into the room, have everyone else sing a chosen song. As the person gets closer to the picture the singing will get louder. If the person starts looking the wrong way the singing will get softer. Take turns having different people leave the room and singing different songs.

COMPANION

Copy this page onto white card stock. Color, cut out, and laminate for longer use. Shrink the picture if you want a smaller object to hide.

"CHOOSE THE RIGHT" GAME

LESSON: The lesson for your Family Home Evening to go with this game should be based on choosing the right. Teach your children that if they pray and study the scriptures they will learn what Heavenly Father wants them to do. Discuss each word strip during the game and how each correct choice will bless your children in their lives.

TO MAKE: Copy the following page of word strips on card stock. Cut them apart, fold them in half, and place them in a bowl. You will need 5 copies of the page of blessing tokens so that you will have enough to hand out during the game. Copy them onto 5 different bright-colored sheets of card stock. Cut them out and laminate for longer use. Copy the die onto another bright sheet of card stock. Laminate and cut out. Fold on the lines and tape together to form the die.

TO PLAY: Place all the word strips in a bowl. Divide into two teams. When the die is rolled and the "blessing" side is up, the team rolling will automatically receive a blessing token. If the "lose a turn" side is up, the team then loses its turn. If the "pencil" is rolled by a team member, that person then draws one of the word strips. He/she will then draw a picture of what is on the word strip. Decide on a time limit. If their teammates can guess what is being drawn in the time frame allotted, they will receive a blessing token. If they can't guess it and the other team can, then the opposing team receives a blessing token. If no one guesses, no token is given. If the "drama masks" are rolled, then a member of the team will choose a word strip. That member then has the same amount of allotted time to act out what is on the word strip. If teammates can guess what was written, they receive a blessing token. If they don't know the answer and the other team can guess what was on the word strip, then they receive the blessing token. Take turns between teams rolling the die. Also make sure each member of each team takes turns drawing or acting. The team with the most blessing tokens at the end of the game is the winner. To play this game over and over you may want to write up your own ideas on word strips. That way, each game will be different, and you won't be playing with the same word strips each time.

Help shovel snow	Pay your tithing	Iron Sunday clothes
Wash the dishes	Bear your testimony	Read your scriptures
Say personal prayers	Write to a missionary	Make cookies to share
Plant a garden	Be baptized	Hold Home Evening
Do homework	Show love to others	Eat healthy foods
Go to bed on time	Get a priesthood blessing	Take the sacrament
Go to the temple	Mow the lawn	Sit reverently in church
Make your bed	Play the piano	Dust the living room
Visit your grandparents	Write in your journal	Bring a friend to church
Read to your little sister	Mop the floor	Set the table
Hold family prayer	Give a talk in church	Rake the leaves
Fast 2 meals	Feed your dog	Do genealogy
Watch conference on TV	Sing at church	Teach a lesson
Take out the garbage	Get up on time	Brush your teeth daily
Change the baby's diaper	Get good grades	Smile at others
Wash the car	Shine Dad's shoes	Fold the laundry
Listen in Primary	Cheer up someone sad	Read the *Friend*
Earn some money	Sweep the floor	Carry groceries for mom
Dress modestly	Hang up your clothes	Think of Christ
Attend church	Share with others	Repent

BLESSING TOKENS

Copy this page onto 5 different bright-colored pieces of card stock. Cut out and laminate for longer use.

DIE

Copy this page onto a bright-colored piece of card stock. Cut out and laminate. Fold on the lines and tape together to form the die.

SABBATH DAY TOSS ACROSS

LESSON: The lesson for your Family Home Evening to go with this game should be based on keeping the Sabbath day holy. Discuss with your family the importance of this commandment and which activities are appropriate and which are not. Teach your family that as they observe this commandment they will feel closer to Heavenly Father and Jesus Christ.

TO MAKE: Copy each of the following pages of floor tiles onto bright-colored card stock. You can make each letter a different color for a brighter game. Cut out each letter and laminate for longer use. For the page of cards at the end of the game, copy them as many times as you will need for each family member to have a set. Make each page a different color. Cut out each card and laminate for longer use. You will need a beanbag for this game. If you don't have one, a rolled up pair of socks will work.

TO PLAY: Lay out all the floor tiles as shown below. Tape the corner of each letter securely to the floor so they will not move as the bean bag lands on them. Put a piece of tape on the floor to mark where to stand to throw the bean bag. You may want to have 2 lines—one for younger members of your family and one for older members. Make a pile of the Sabbath Day spelling cards for each family member. Starting with the youngest member of your family, take turns tossing the beanbag on the floor tile letters. For each letter that is landed on, family members get a card from their pile to spell out the word SABBATH DAY. If a player lands on a letter and no longer needs that letter, the player passes the bean bag to the next player. Remember that you will need to land on the "A" 3 times the "B" 2 times, and the other letters only need to be landed on once. When a family member has gotten all of the cards in his pile to spell out the words "SABBATH DAY" that member is the winner.

FLOOR TILES

Copy this page onto bright card stock. You can use a different color for each floor tile letter. Cut out and laminate for longer use.

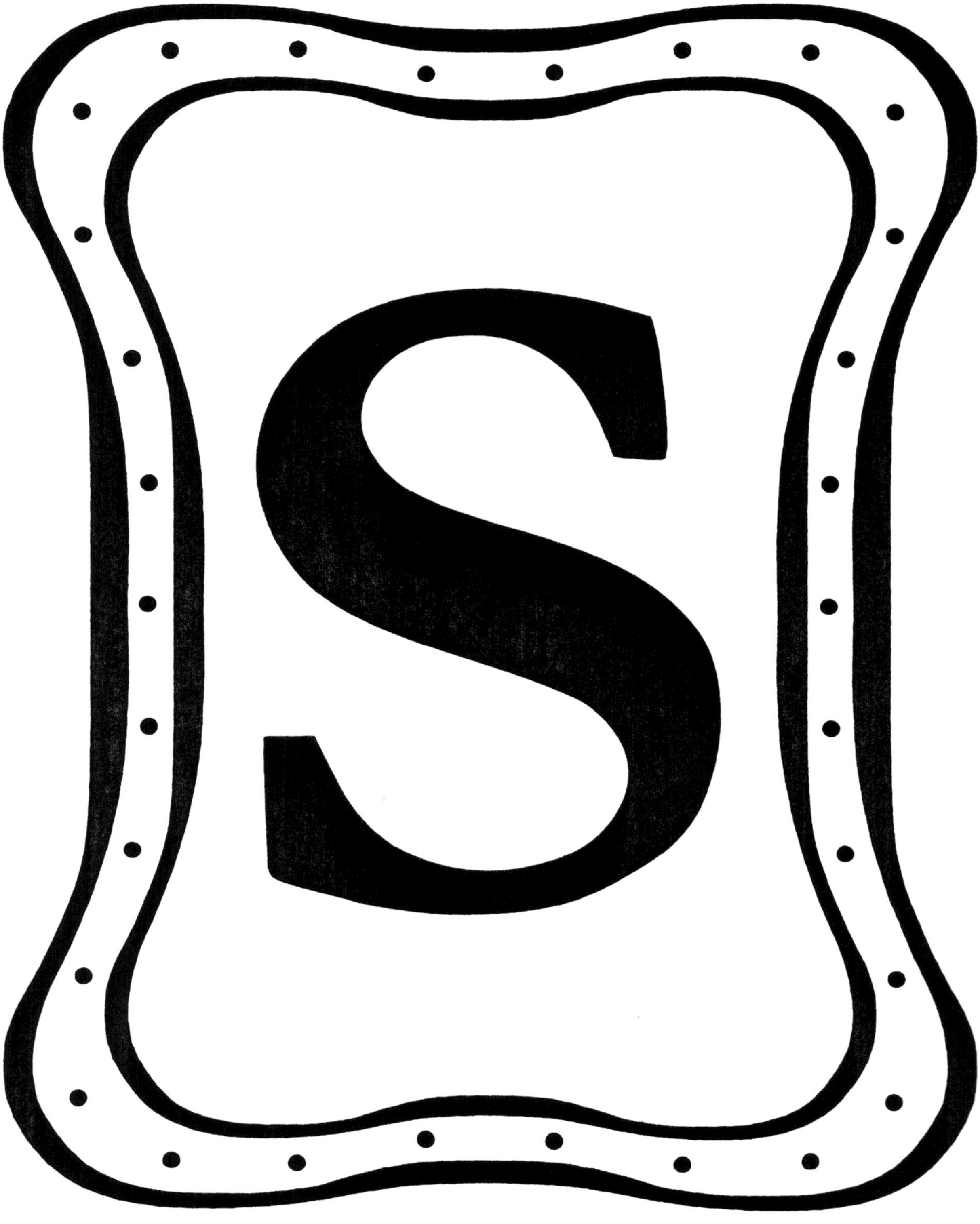

FLOOR TILES

Copy this page onto bright card stock. You can use a different color for each floor tile letter. Cut out and laminate for longer use.

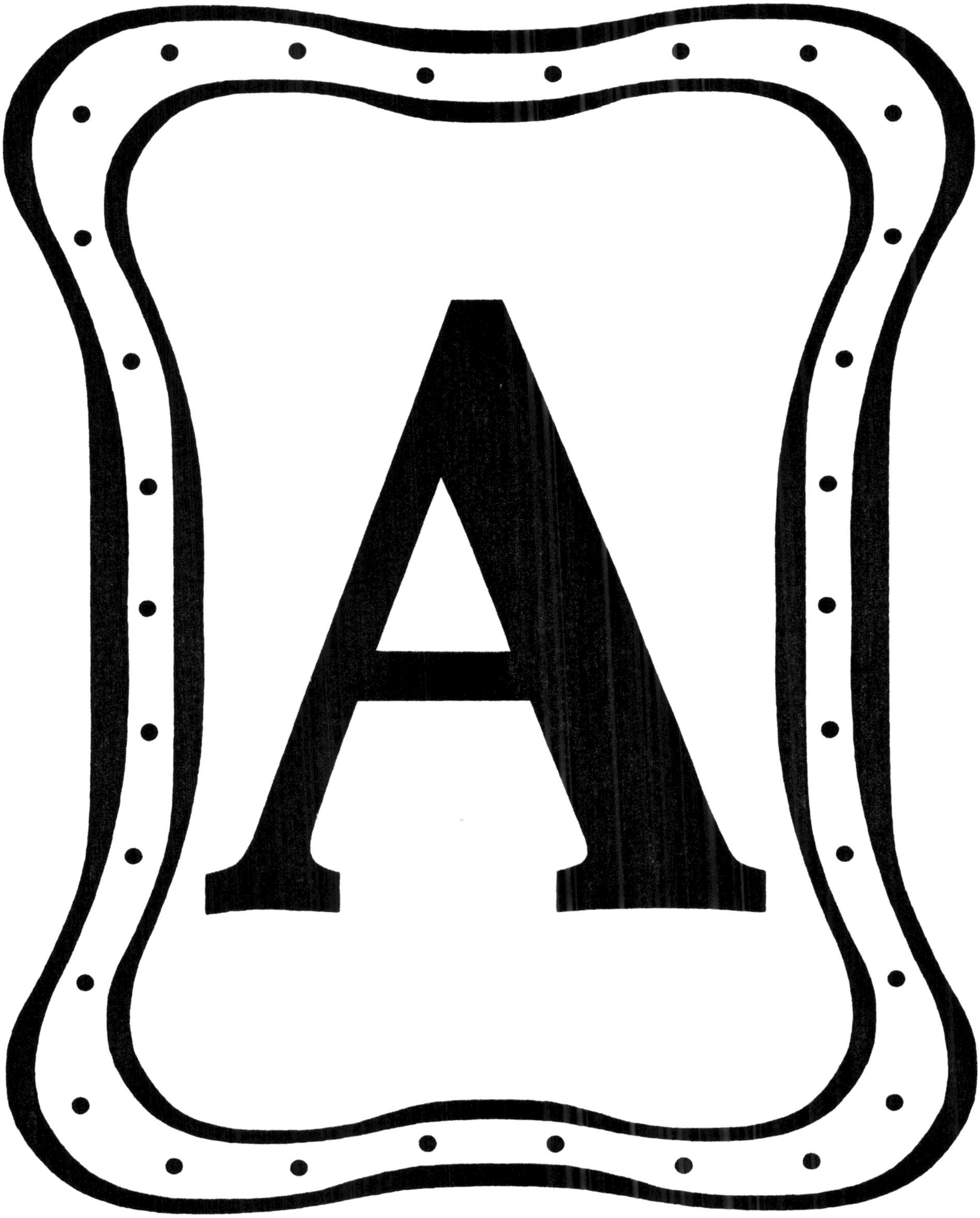

FLOOR TILES

Copy this page onto bright card stock. You can use a different color for each floor tile letter. Cut out and laminate for longer use.

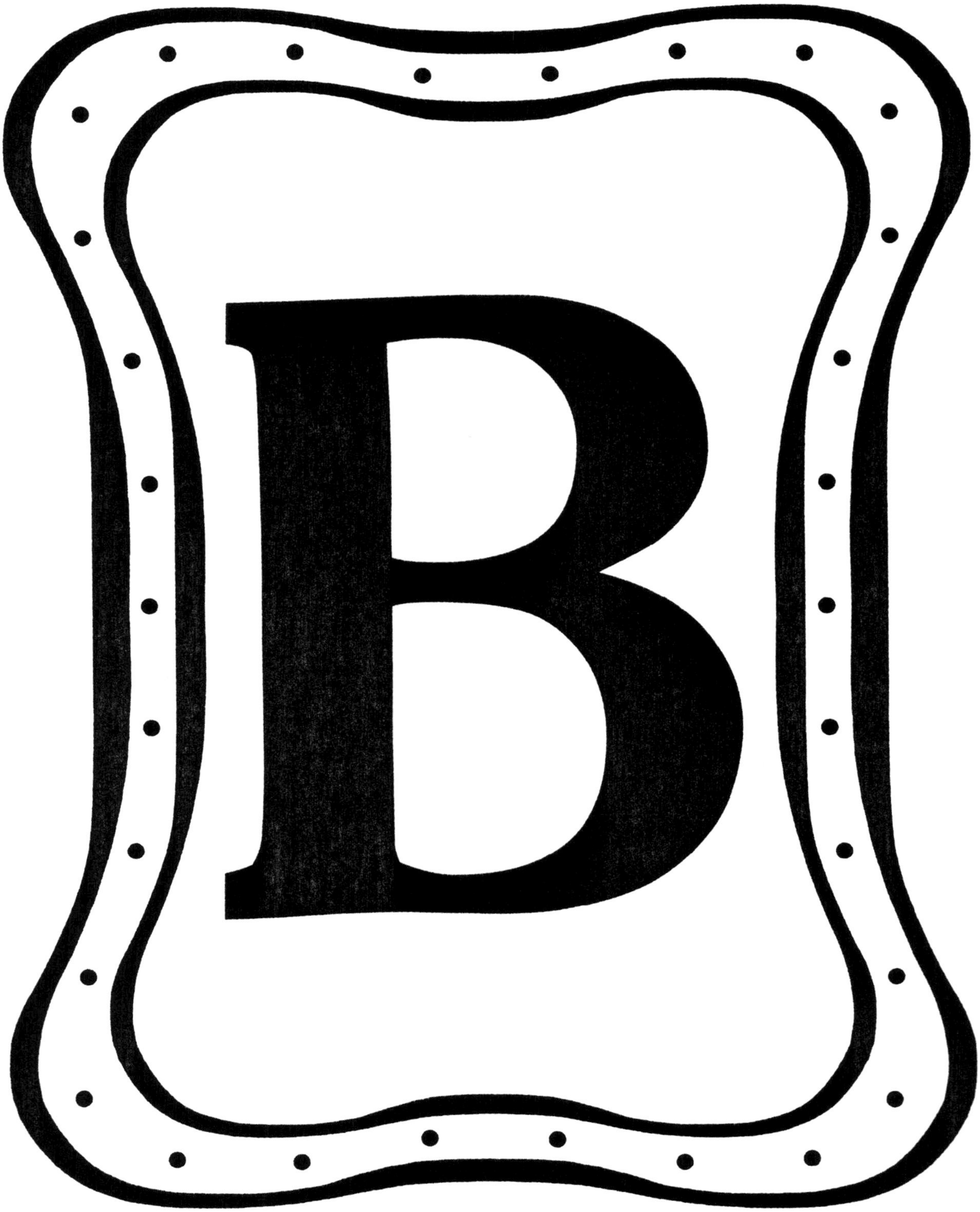

FLOOR TILES

Copy this page onto bright card stock. You can use a different color for each floor tile letter. Cut out and laminate for longer use.

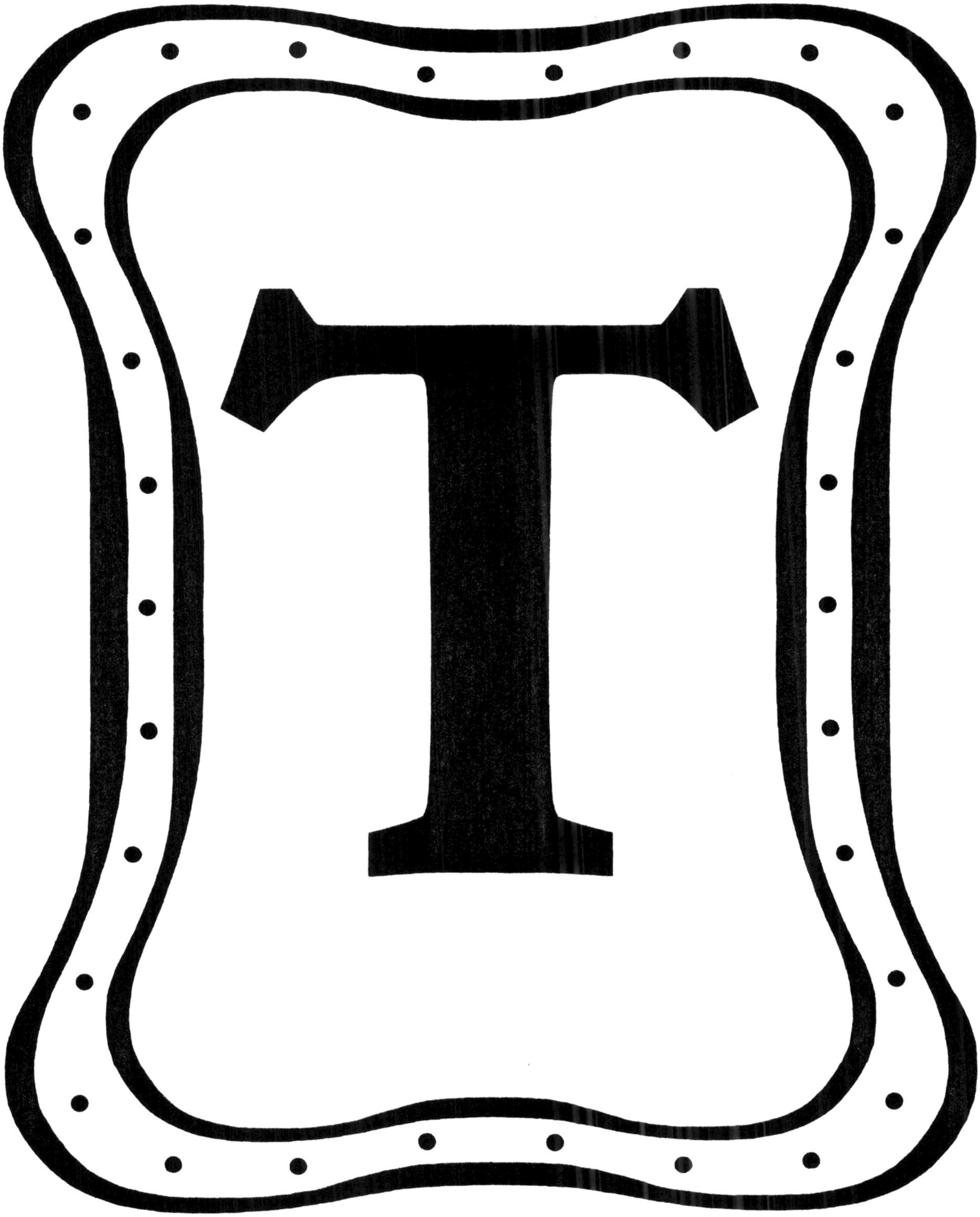

FLOOR TILES

Copy this page onto bright card stock. You can use a different color for each floor tile letter. Cut out and laminate for longer use.

FLOOR TILES

Copy this page onto bright card stock. You can use a different color for each floor tile letter. Cut out and laminate for longer use.

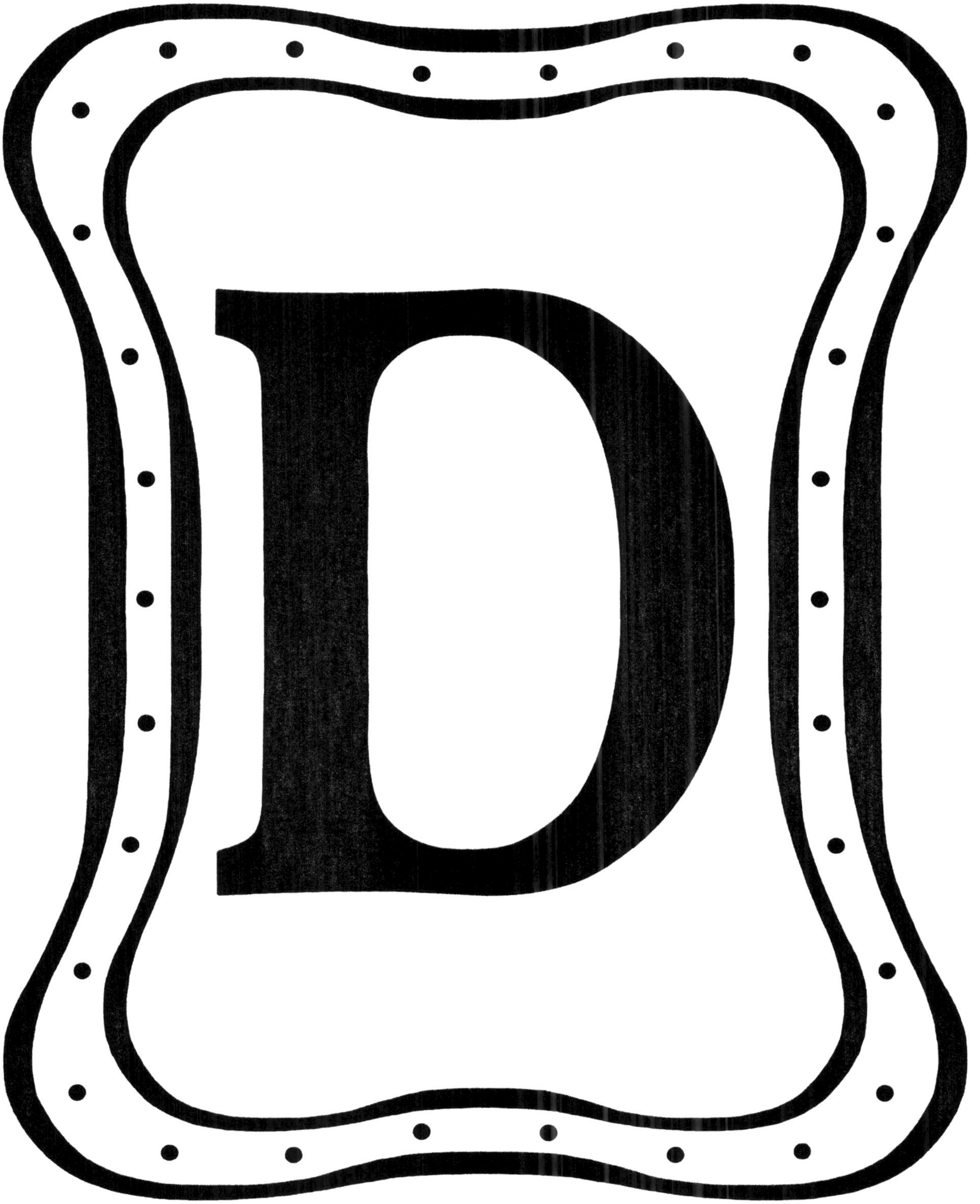

FLOOR TILES

Copy this page onto bright card stock. You can use a different color for each floor tile letter. Cut out and laminate for longer use.

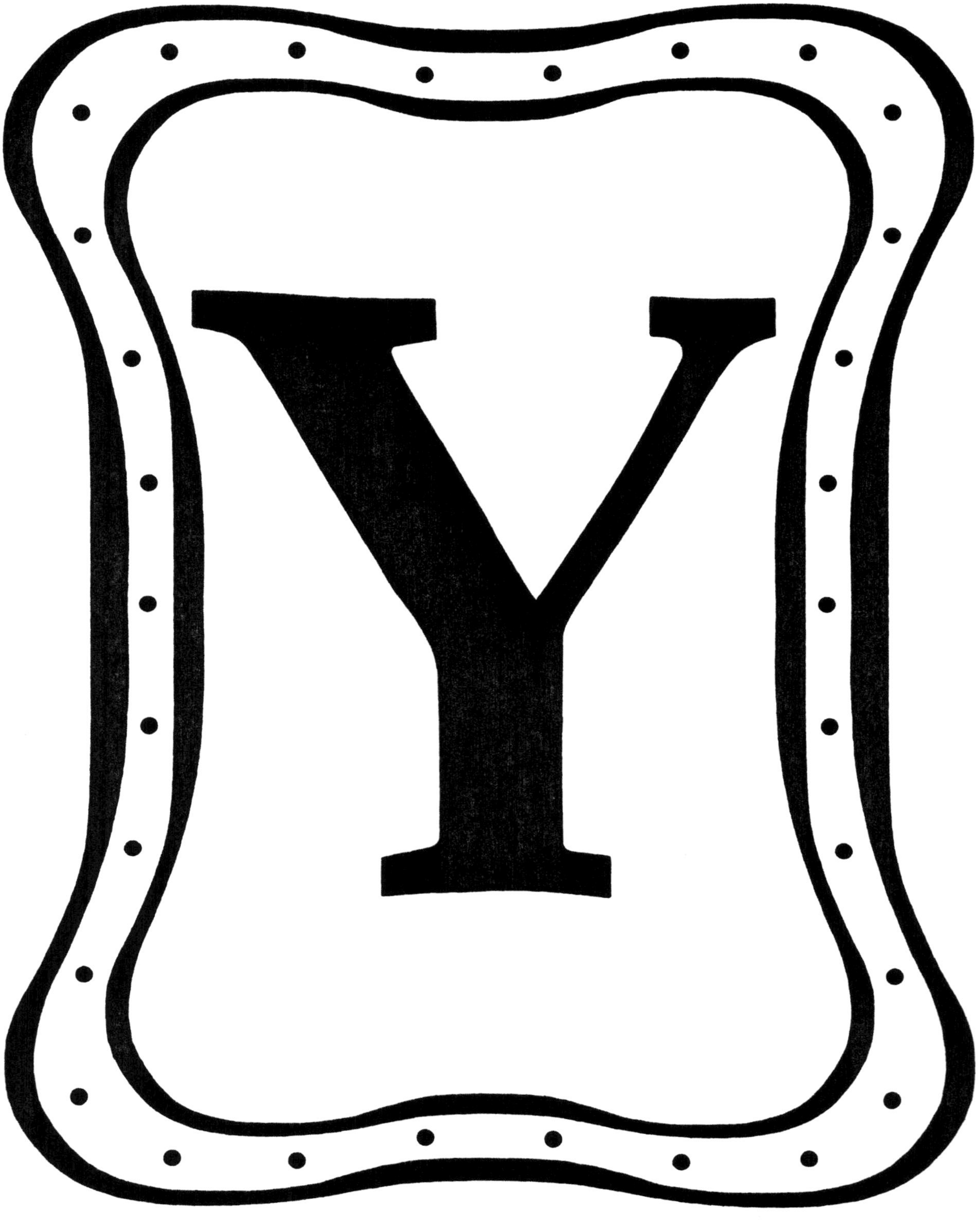

SPELLING CARDS

Copy this page onto bright card stock for each member of your family. Use a different color for each family member. Cut out and laminate for longer use.

S

A B B

A T H

D A Y

SECRET SERVICE GAME

LESSON: The lesson for your Family Home Evening to go with this game should be about the importance of service. Discuss with your family how you can teach the gospel through serving others. Also talk about the importance of giving service gladly and watching for ways that you can help others each day. Explain how you can start with your own family by doing small acts of service every day for each other. Tell your children how fun it is to do secret acts of service for other members of the family.

TO MAKE: Copy the following page as many times as you need for clues in your treasure hunt. You can copy them on white card stock and color them or copy them onto bright-colored card stock. On the back of each treasure hunt clue, write hints to have the children look in places where they could be helpful, such as "Mom needs help drying the dishes," and then hide the next clue in the dish towel drawer. Copy the page with the large "Secret Service Agent" one time on white card stock and color it, or copy it onto bright-colored card stock. Cut out and laminate.

TO PLAY: Hide all your clues prior to Family Home Evening. Instead of hiding a clue in the last place, hide your refreshments. After you have finished your lesson, tell the children that you are going to have a "Service Treasure Hunt." Give the children the first clue and tell them to think of where they would have to go to find something to help with that clue. At the end of the game and after the refreshments have been served, tell the children that you are going to continue to play throughout the week by using the larger "Secret Service Agent" picture. Start with one member of the family. Have them do a "Secret Service" for another member of the family and then leave the "Secret Service Agent." When that person finds the "Secret Service Agent" and sees what has been done, they then do a "Secret Service" for another family member and leaves the "Secret Service Agent" for that person to pass on another act of service. Continue doing this game all through the next week. In the lesson the following week, discuss how much fun it was to secretly do acts of service and how it made them feel.

I CAN BE A SECRET SERVICE AGENT

TREASURE HUNT CLUES

Copy this page onto bright card stock for as many clues as you need for your treasure hunt. Cut out and laminate for longer use.

SECRET SERVICE AGENT

Copy this page onto white card stock and color or onto bright card stock. Cut out and laminate for longer use.

GRATITUDE DOMINOES

LESSON: The lesson for your Family Home Evening to go with this game should be about gratitude for the plan of salvation. Talk about the wonderful opportunity that Heavenly Father has given us to come to this beautiful world to learn and grow. Discuss how grateful we are for Jesus Christ and his atonement. Also talk about the gratitude we have for Joseph Smith and the restoration of the Church to the earth again, and the gratitude we have for living prophets today. Before playing the game, talk about each of the pictures on the dominoes and how each picture relates to your lesson.

TO MAKE: Copy the following pages of dominoes onto different colored card stock. Cut out each domino and laminate for longer use.

TO PLAY: Lay all the dominoes face down and off to the side. Have each family member draw 5 dominoes and either place them face down on the table in front of them or hold them like cards so no one else can see them. Start with the youngest player. Have them choose one of their dominoes and lay it down in the middle of the table. Then, going by age (to make it easier, sit in order by age), have each player lay down a match to the domino that has been played. If the player does not have a match, they then have to draw from the pile until they get a match, and then they lay it down. All the dominoes drawn are then added to their hand. Matching dominoes can be laid on any side of the domino as shown below. When a double picture domino is laid down, it forms a T and can be added on to from all 4 sides of the domino, as shown below. Continue taking turns and playing until someone lays down all their dominoes and becomes the winner.

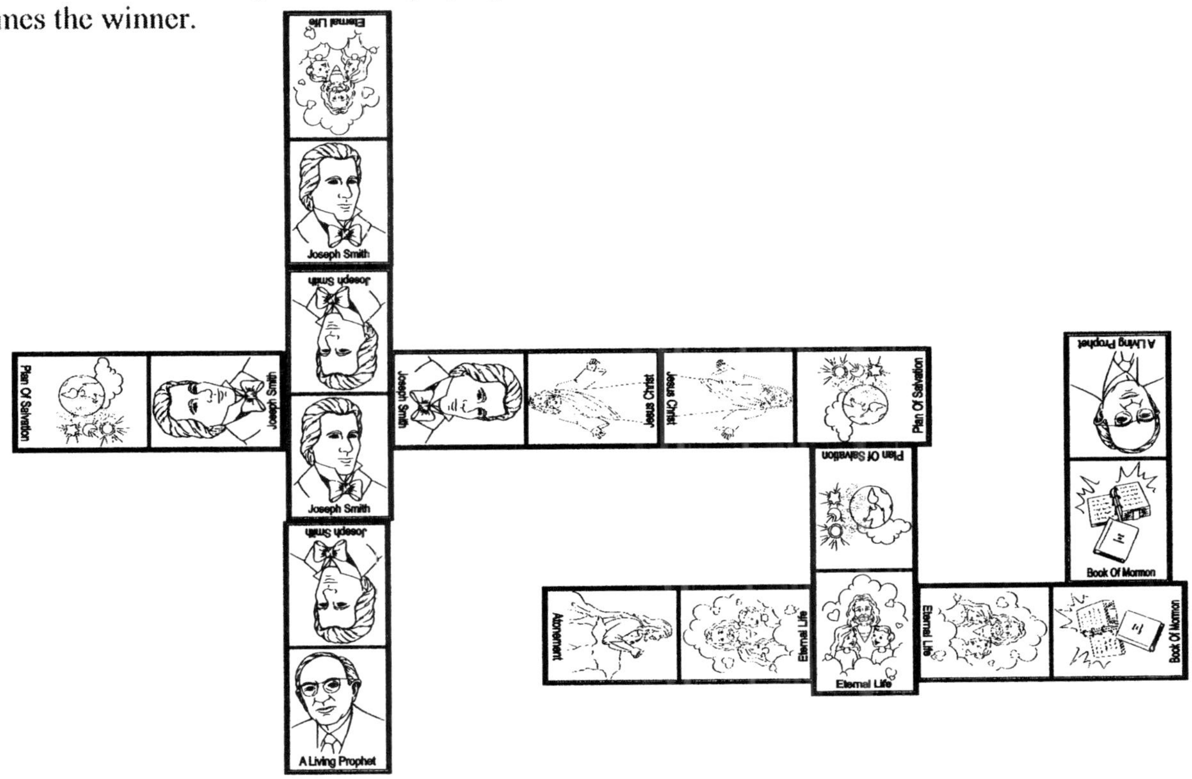

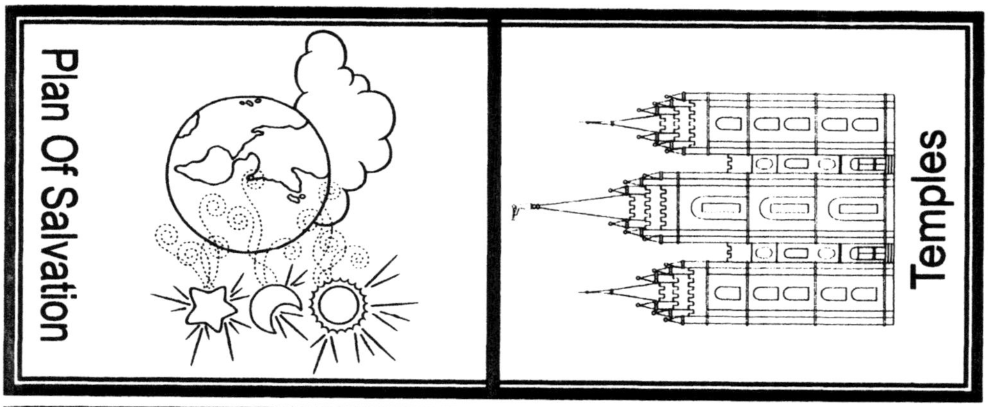

DOMINOES

Copy this page onto bright card stock. Cut out each double picture domino and laminate for longer use.

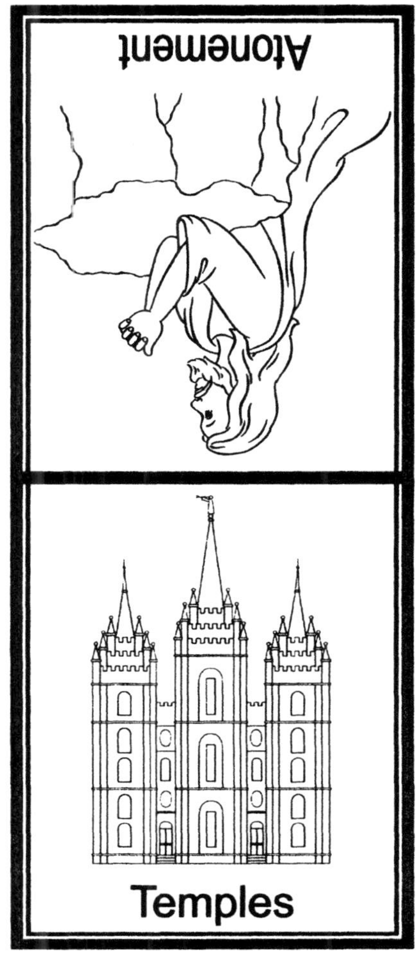

DOMINOES

Copy this page onto bright card stock. Cut out each double picture domino and laminate for longer use.

DOMINOES

Copy this page onto bright card stock. Cut out each double picture domino and laminate for longer use.

DOMINOES

Copy this page onto bright card stock. Cut out each double picture domino and laminate for longer use.

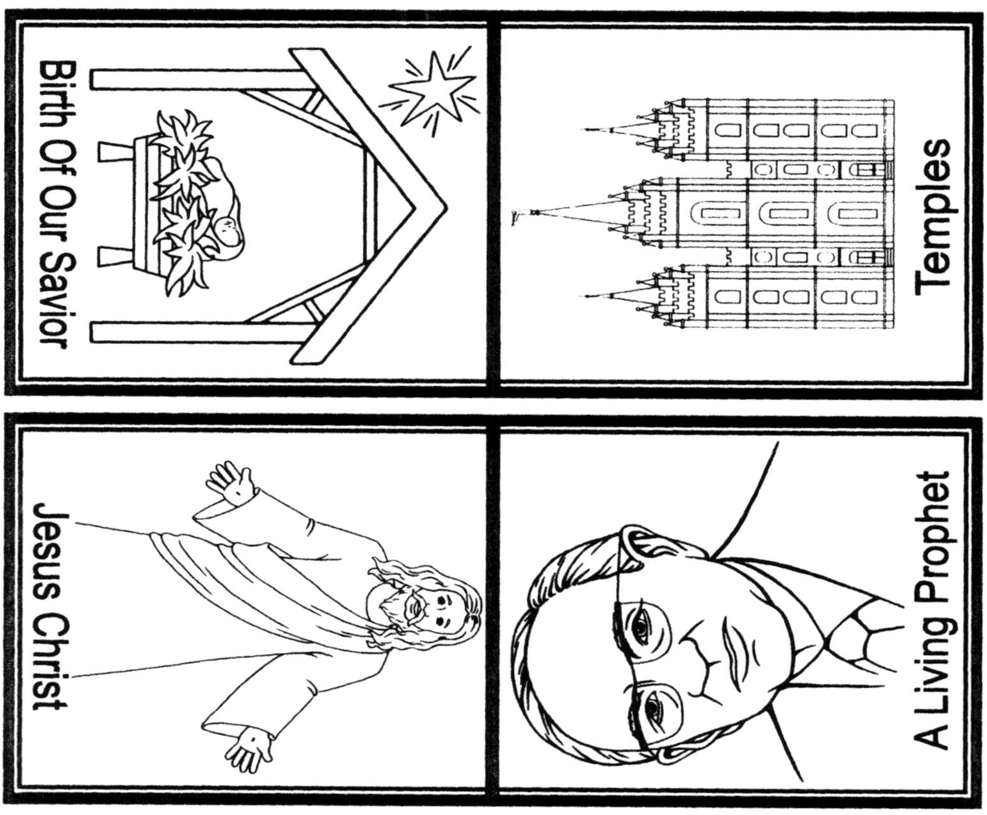

DOMINOES

Copy this page onto bright card stock. Cut out each double picture domino and laminate for longer use.

DOMINOES

Copy this page onto bright card stock. Cut out each double picture domino and laminate for longer use.

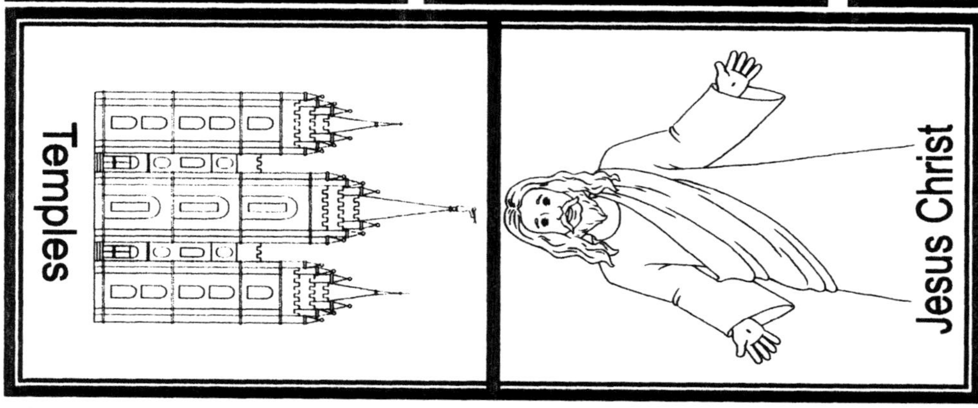

DOMINOES

Copy this page onto bright card stock. Cut out each double picture domino and laminate for longer use.

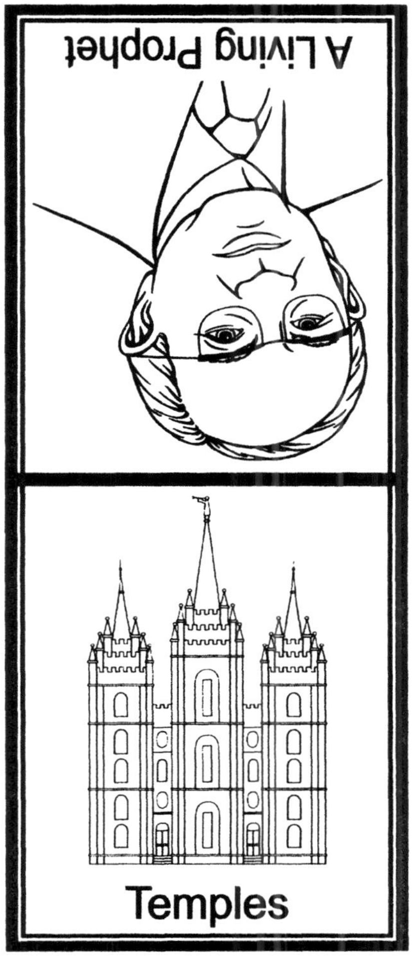

DOMINOES

Copy this page onto bright card stock. Cut out each double picture domino and laminate for longer use.

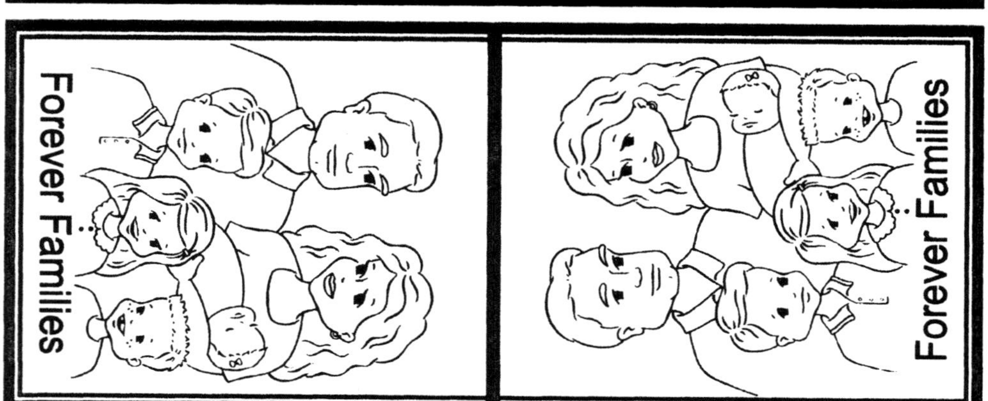

DOMINOES

Copy this page onto bright card stock. Cut out each double picture domino and laminate for longer use.

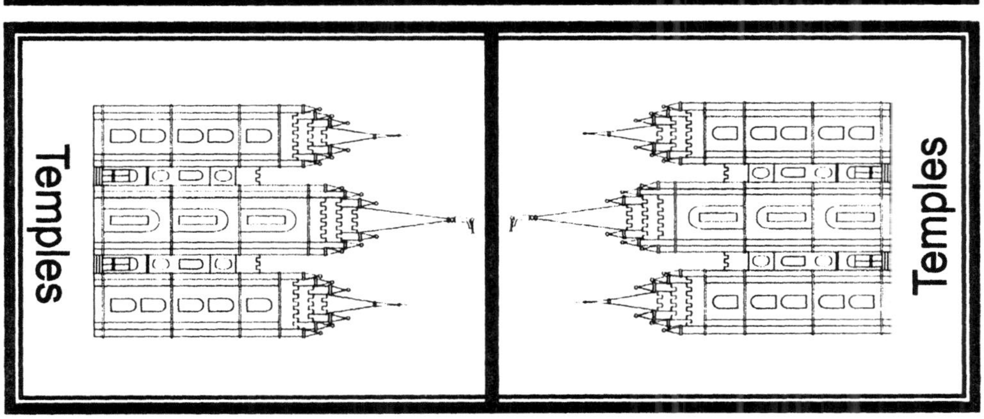

DOMINOES

Copy this page onto bright card stock. Cut out each double picture domino and laminate for longer use.